SET READY
By MICHAEL PARNALL

Am I The Idiot On Set?
Copyright © 2018 by Michael Parnall

All rights reserved. No part of this publication may be reproduced, distributed, or transmitted in any form or by any means, including photocopying, recording, or other electronic or mechanical methods, without the prior written permission of the author, except in the case of brief quotations embodied in critical reviews and certain other non-commercial uses permitted by copyright law.

editing by Michelle Cornish
tonsofproductions.com
amitheidiotonset@gmail.com

Tellwell Talent
www.tellwell.ca

ISBN
978-0-2288-0566-3 (Paperback)
978-1-77527-781-1 (eBook)

Dedicated to
Danny Berre Parnall

TABLE OF CONTENTS

Preface.. vii

Chapter 1: The Five Most Important Rules.......... 1

Chapter 2: Walkie Talkie on a Film Set............ 17

Chapter 3: Slang Words 23

Chapter 4: Department Names...................... 33

Chapter 5: General Requirements 47

Epilogue.. 59

Thank You 61

About the Author 72

PREFACE

Idiotic [Id-ee-ot-ik]:
"Senselessly foolish or stupid."
(www.dictionary.com)

There were many times when I started doing film work that left me feeling like an idiot because I didn't know the proper terminology. This is something I want to help new crew members avoid because it is an example where ignorance is not bliss! I wish there was a reference book available when I started working in this industry years ago.

It is not my intention to claim that these are rules listed by a film school or a set etiquette course, but from my own experience working in the industry for ten plus years. I personally know people starting in the industry who would be saved the embarrassment of ignorance, and crew members who would be saved the frustration of constantly correcting others because of the rules and lists that are contained within.

The first things I list in this book are five imperative rules that apply to every movie set worldwide, and the meanings for each one. There are too many stories for me to share them all, so I will focus on the important ones. I want newbies to understand why breaking one of these rules would be so embarrassing for them and costly to the film production.

In the second chapter, I describe how to use a walkie-talkie, so a new crew member feels less intimidated.

The third chapter is a list of the slang words used by crew members in Vancouver B.C.

In the fourth chapter, I list the job titles for crew you may encounter on an active film set. There are several job titles that never come to the actual set, so I left them out of the identifications.

Finally, in the fifth chapter I list the not-so-stringent rules that if followed will make the process of working on a film set run smoothly. A lot of these instructions will seem like common sense to some, but not all sense is common to everyone. When anything seems obvious to most crew members, new or stupid people can overlook it because they're not paying attention. Each person can only claim to be new a few times and after that they will be considered a knuckle-dragging, drooling, low IQ, idiot. I know that sounds harsh but make no mistake about it; the film industry can be a cut throat business that should never be taken lightly.

1
The Five Most Important Rules

RULE #1. - BE ON TIME!!

I can't emphasize this enough and I know it is the golden rule for any job. We have been told our entire lives that if we are late too often it could cost us our job, and no one wants to be fired. When they say in film you must be on time it means more than just in the morning. You must be on time in a whole host of ways because a film set is all about timing. If you work on a television show or feature film set it can cost from one hundred to five hundred dollars per minute depending on the show. Every department on set works together as a machine, and if they all must wait because anyone is late for any reason, then that person is called an idiot!

It also doesn't matter what department anyone works for either. If the props person gets the props late to set making everyone wait, then that person is called an idiot. If the main actor has a long lunch and everyone has an obligation to wait until they get to set, then the actor is an idiot. If a revised version of the script would show up in the morning on the day of shooting, then that means the writers changed their minds about some of the dialog. The actors must memorize changes at the last minute, so now the writers are a group of idiots, or the plural: "idieye". Any time one person halts the momentum of the filming machine, they will be called an idiot by a lot of people on the set. Never think any crew are above being called this when it comes to being late.

While working for a popular television show I experienced the gravity of this vital instruction. On this occasion, there was a stand-in actor that would always disrupt the flow of filming because of his constant tardiness. It wasn't just in the morning but every time he was needed on set. It was astonishing that he could continue to work for the show for that long. I found out it was because this was the person they had used since day one and they didn't want to hurt his feelings. It was the seventh year that he was on the show and had made a great number of friends. It had become obvious that he had lost all interest in the show and took the job for granted. He was not invited back for the next season because it became too much for the producers to handle.

I know this story lacks the "WOW" factor but it shows what becoming complacent can do to anyone's career. He lost the sense of urgency that accompanies the continuous attention this job requires. The stand-in actors who I watched become successful actors eventually, were the ones who read the script and acted like an understudy in stage acting. They stayed engaged in the filming process and this helped them gain acting strength. If interest and passion are gone then it isn't long until the person will be ejected from the job and sometimes from film forever.

This rule is just as important to every crew member in the entire production. Each department is their own team, and work with all the other teams at the same time. For example, if the construction dept. is not finished an installation on time, it can throw off the next departments to do their jobs according to the schedule. The painters are delayed, the set decorators are behind, so on and so on. To be on time is a requirement, not an option. If you or your team is late most of the time the production will find people who are not late.

RULE #2. - BE QUIET!!

TURN OFF YOUR CELL PHONE WHEN WORKING ON THE SET!

When any crew member ignores this regulation, it can cost the production a lot of money. The microphones used for filming are very sensitive and can pick up almost any sound. If they are filming a perfect take of a scene and it is interrupted by the sound of a slamming door, then they must film it again. Like I said in the first rule, time is money so if they unnecessarily refilm the scene because someone screwed it up by making noise, then that person is an idiot. It doesn't matter how loud the noise is, be aware that the microphones will pick it up. From opening a bag of chips, to doing the zipper up on a coat, walking on a hard wood surface, basically any noise no matter how small will be detected.

Talking is the big culprit for many idiots. When you hear "ROLLING" over the radio or from a Production

Am I The Idiot?

Assistant yelling it then shut your mouth. Anyone who talks on channel one after the first Assistant Director says "Rolling", or before saying "Cut", should be prepared for the worst. Do not whisper or think they can't hear you because if they can than you are an idiot.

Back in the day I was working as a Production Assistant (PA) on a feature film and was stationed near the cameras. I yelled "ROLLING" when it came over the radio while some grips who were standing close to me kept talking loudly. I asked them to please be quiet for the scene and they gave me attitude. One of them told me it didn't matter because I would be the one bitched at. I replied that I am the voice of the first AD, so I guess I should just tell him that you don't care about his sound. Their eyes went wide, and they took off back to their truck. I am not a rat but come on! If you think I am taking the wrap for you because you don't care, then I will make sure that everyone knows who the idiot is. My job description as a PA. does not include covering for idiots!

Many times, I witnessed our location department being asked to do ridiculous things for the sound. Once we were filming near the airport and the sound got interrupted by overhead planes landing and taking off all day long. The first AD requested that the location department call the airport to reroute the planes for them or get the schedule for the day. We all laughed but I think the AD was serious. There is only so much that can be done when it comes to fixing the sound.

I had another experience on a set in the suburbs filming on a low budget feature film. We were about four hours into the film day when a construction site three blocks away started to saw stone for the driveway. It was very loud, and our sound department started to complain. I was asked to go over to the site and find out if they could stop for the day. They didn't seem to care about our sound because of their schedule, and it would cost a lot of money to stop their progress. They finally agreed to only use the saw between scenes when we were cut. I had to stand there and yell "ROLLING" and "CUT" to the construction workers for the rest of the day. This was a day when working in film was not so glamorous, let me tell you.

RULE #3. - PAY ATTENTION!!

This is another big rule that everyone should follow and not just because of the time wasted, but because it can cause a lot of bad things to happen. From spilling your drink on expensive equipment, to being seen in the shot, or parking your car in the wrong place. Basically, any time anybody is not paying attention they can become the idiot. When someone gets hurt or dies on set because they were not paying attention this is the worst thing I have seen. What's even sadder is the person who got hurt or died because they were not paying attention, are always remembered as an idiot. No one wants to be that person. Ouch!!

There are many other reasons to be the idiot that did not pay attention. There was a time when I was doing background acting on a big movie set. They were set up for the shot and they noticed a PA standing to the right of the frame. He was talking on his cell phone and not really paying attention to what was going on. The first AD talked to him directly on the radio and asked if he could move twenty steps to his right to get out of the frame. The PA waved his hand and walked off set.

The AD yelled "rolling" over the radio and the scene started. A few minutes later the same PA talking on his phone walked back on to set. He was wearing a reflective vest and forced the AD to yell "CUT", stopping the whole scene. The First AD started to yell at the PA on the walkie-talkie, "What are you doing?" The P.A. waved his hand slinking off the set once he realized that there were eighty people looking at him.

The AD screamed back to starting positions and we all went back to where we started to do the scene. Yelling "action" started all the people to come to life once more. The scene was long and about half-way through when the exact same PA walked onto set talking on his phone again. The AD was now beside himself furious screaming "CUT"! The AD marched from his spot beside the camera over to the PA that was standing about fifty feet away, grabbed the cell phone out of the PA's hand, and threw it into the dark woods. He looked the PA in the eyes and yelled "GET OFF MY SET"! I know he was called a lot worse than an idiot that day.

RULE #4. - DON'T GUESS!!

If a crew member is doing any job on set it is imperative to know what to do. Sometimes there are a lot of things to accomplish and if the boss gives several instructions then everything must be completed as directed. My advice is to always have a note book to write the orders down if the list gets too long. How smart anyone thinks they are is irrelevant because everyone forgets sometimes, and that results in being thought of as an idiot.

Every piece of equipment used on a movie set is for a specific purpose. From guessing if it is okay to charge your phone in a socket, to whether it is the right trailer to go into, or leaving all your gear in the wrong place, all result in the wrong action. If you don't ask someone because you aren't sure, then you could be labeled an idiot.

A few years ago, I was working as a PA on a television show. The person in charge asked me and three other guys to set up a lunch room for everyone. We were told to carry twenty-five eight-foot tables up two flights of stairs to the room we were to use. Each table had eight chairs to go with it as well. After we set them all up we were told to go to different lock-ups around the set. About an hour later I was called on the radio to come back to the lunch room. When I got there, I was told that we set up the wrong room and we had to break down all the tables and chairs. Then we had to carry them all back down the stairs to another room in the building. It turns out that the one in charge of us forgot which room and guessed. It wasn't just me and the guys who thought he was an idiot, but his boss also called him an idiot! If you cause unnecessary work because you guessed, then you will be considered an idiot for sure.

RULE #5. - BE RESPECTFUL

I know the title of this rule is contradictory because calling someone an idiot is not respectful. What I mean is be respectful to keep drama amongst the crew at a minimum. The crew on any set works together as a team, keep in mind that a lot of this crew has not slept properly, are under pressure, and dealing with several people. I think the best way to deal with this is to not take anything personally if anyone talks to you in a rude way. I know it can be hard to do but it takes away the emotional reaction that can ruin your long day.

The other thing that will help is keeping your opinion that someone is an idiot to yourself unless you are their boss. When any of these rules are broken, the person who did it already knows they are an idiot or will soon find out from their superior. If you show up on time, be quiet, pay attention, don't guess, and are respectful to people then you will avoid being the known idiot.

Am I The Idiot?

I have experienced a lot of people who are disrespectful to the people they work with. Once as a background actor I worked with this older guy for three days. He would always lose props and wardrobe given to him by the production team. The pretty young girls that were there had to deal with this guy flirting with them constantly, even on set. Offering them a massage or always eavesdropping on their conversations. He would fill his bag with food from craft services and throw his garbage on the ground. He is known by many in the film industry as an idiot and was banned to work on many shows.

This rule is also known amongst the crew members. Each department can work together for long periods of time and some crew members become friends because of this. When these people poke fun at and rib their workmates it is tolerated to a degree. Bullying or incessant teasing is never tolerated and can result in being fired.

One of the mistakes that new members can make is to not show the actors the respect they need. The reason is they are trying to maintain a character, and some can be thrown off focus if made to socially interact with the crew. They are trying to remember the order of the dialogue they memorized and if you are the one to make them forget than expect to be called an idiot. It is not that the actors think they are better than anyone and it is not personal. I have been asked many times over the years not to make eye contact with certain actors and it is a common requirement in some productions. All our jobs rely on the ability of the actors so PLEASE only talk to them if they talk to you first.

Each set has different rules that are considered important. I left the next few pages blank to write down the rules not listed.

~ DON'T FORGET THESE RULES!!! ~

~ DON'T FORGET THESE RULES!!! ~

~ DON'T FORGET THESE RULES!!! ~

~ DON'T FORGET THESE RULES!!! ~

2
Walkie Talkie on a Film Set

The walkie-talkie is a tool used by almost everyone on the film crew. Most have fifteen frequency channels. Each channel is assigned to a specific purpose and is displayed on the call sheet most of the time. Every show decides what each channel is to be used for, and it is the responsibility of each of the crew members to be aware of this before they work on that set. Being respectful is the job of each crew member when using the walkie, and to make clear they understand how to use it. I will give an example of the channel assignments from one show I worked on. I must reiterate that the order or assignments are different for each show.

Channel 1: General Production - The first AD uses this channel to direct the crew as the filming is being completed. This is also the open channel that is used for the crew to get each other's attention. This channel is never to be used to have a conversation amongst the crew; it is just to call attention to other crew members. One of the golden rules applied to this channel is to never talk on this channel after the First AD says "rolling" or before he says "cut". Swearing and using foul language on this channel is an offense that can be met with a fine and/or the offender being fired. Breaking any of these rules will result in several crew members thinking you are an idiot. They may think it to themselves or say it directly to you.

Channel 2: This is an open talk channel that is used for short conversations. If the first AD is using this channel, then any crew member must wait until they are done before continuing. The conversations on this channel are to be brief and direct. If the conversation requires a longer exchange, then it must be conducted on the fifth channel. When the conversation is completed it is good practice to remind the other crew member to go back to channel one.

Channel 3: Camera Department.

Channel 4: Lighting Department.

Channel 5: This is an open channel that any of the crew can use. When a conversation between crew members is a longer exchange they should use this channel.

Channel 6: Sound Department.

Channel 7: Grips Department.

Channel 8: Rigging Department.

Channel 9: Props Department.

Channel 10: Transport Department.

Channel 11: Special Effects Department

Channel 12: Locations Department

Communicating on the walkie-talkie is one skill that takes practice and over time becomes second nature. The formal rule of saying "Over" when you finish talking does not apply all the time. This is the rule in Vancouver Canada, so I cannot speak for other parts of the world. When someone calls you on the walkie it is customary for the person to say your first and last name, or your first name and department.

For example, when I was working as a PA, or in Locations then people would say, "Mike, Locations" on channel one to get my attention. I would reply, "Go for Mike" as a response and the person calling me would then tell me what channel I was to change to. I would turn the dial to the appropriate number and repeat, "Go for Mike". The conversation at that point was more relaxed and we could talk freely. When the conversation is finished each of the participants should say, "Back to one" to remind each other to change their walkie-talkie back to Channel One. I don't know how many times I have forgotten to change it back and I could not hear when I was being called because I was still on Channel Five.

I know using the walkie-talkie can be a bit intimidating at first but eventually it will become a useful tool to get the work done quicker. It is good to remember that if you are working on an active film set this means there are between thirty and forty crew members, on average, listening to everything you say. The number can be much more if the production is a large one.

The biggest one I ever worked on was about three hundred people if I had to guess, and that would mean at least half or more of those were on Channel One. The reason I mention this is because if you were to do or say something stupid on the live walkie then in one split-second there would be several crew members all thinking, "What an Idiot!". Don't let this frighten you, just be aware of this fact when you do converse on the walkie so that you do it with care.

Each Film Set has different assignments on each walkie channel. The following is left blank, so you can write down the proper list for the set you are working on.

1.

2.

3.

4.

5.

6.

7.

8.

9.

10.

11.

12.

13.

14.

15.

3
Slang Words
(Vancouver, BC, Canada)

Like in any workplace, there is a list of slang words used by the crew. These vary in different parts of the world, so I am only aware of the slang used in Vancouver, Canada.

Abby Singer (Abby): The second from last shot of the film day.

Apple Box (Apple): A solid wooden box of various sizes used on set. Sizes include Full, Half, Quarter, and Pancake.

Blocking: Deciding the placement and movement of the actor, camera, and microphone for each scene.

Booked: Scheduled to work.

Call Sheet: This is a sheet of paper containing all the important information needed for that filming day.

Cast: The principle actors that play in the filmed scenes for each day.

Catering: This is usually a food truck that makes breakfast and lunch each day for the entire cast/crew.

Circus: The group of trailers required by all the film departments. This is usually where catering is set up for meals.

Check the Gate: A part of the camera lens is checked with a flashlight for small hair or dust.

Coke and a Smoke: Take a fifteen minute or more break.

Copy That: I understand what you mean. On the walkie-talkie, some crew just say, "Copy" to save time.

Crafty (Craft Service): A tent with drinks and snacks for all crew members and union actors on set. Non-union background actors have their own Crafty that is only for them to use.

Crew Member: An individual that works behind the camera for the film production.

Crew Call: The time a crew member or actor must be on the film set that day.

Crew Park: Where all the film crew park their personal cars. They are usually watched by a PA or a teamster security officer.

Cut: The filming of one take for a scene is completed.

Day Call: Crew member that only works for one day or limited amount of days.

Eyes On (Visual On): When a crew member says, "I have eyes on", it means they are looking at the person or item required.

Fire Watch: A PA watches the active set during lunch break and reports any problems if they arise.

First Position (Ones): Where main actors, background actors, or vehicles start in a scene.

First Team: The actors in the scene filming at the time.

Final Touches (Last Looks): The makeup and hair artists do their final adjustments to the actors right before filming.

Flying in: Will be on set fast.

Fraterday: When a crew call is Friday night and filming won't finish until Saturday morning.

French Hours: During the film day there is no breaks and the crew eats while working so the day is shorter than normal.

Gak: All the tools and gear of each department.

Genny: Electric generator.

Go For [NAME]: Response when a crew member is called on the radio.

Good Gate: The scene has been filmed properly and is complete.

Hard Eight: Work only an eight-hour shift.

Hold the Roll: Pause the filming for a moment.

Holding: It is where the Extras or Background actors sit.

Honey Wagon: The trailer that has men's and women's washrooms plus the AD department's office. This is where all the paperwork on the filming location is conducted and is an extension of the production office.

Hot Set: Everything on the set is continuity and not to be moved while crew is on break.

Last Man: The last person on the crew has received lunch so the time for lunch break can begin.

Lock Up: A location on the film set that must have a person stand guard.

Mortgage Burner: Working with a production on a show full time during the whole season.

Moving On: Finished filming that scene and moving gear to set up for the next scene.

Picture's Up: An alert for everyone involved to get ready to shoot the scene.

Put-put: A small electric generator.

Rolling: The camera has started filming.

Second Team: The stand in for the actors on set.

Show Call: A crew member hired to work for the entire length of the production's filming schedule. If it is a television show, then the length of a "Show Call" is for the year or season only.

Slating: Video and sound marker using a clap board for the scene identification when editing.

Speeding: The audio equipment has started recording.

Spell off: Relief on a location on set that must be guarded the whole film day.

Stand by: Please wait until you are needed. This also applies to objects to be used soon or brought nearby just in case they are needed.

Talent: Actors

Ten-one: Go to the washroom.

Turning around: Moving the entire camera and lighting set up to film the same scene from a different angle.

Two Holler: Trailer with two doors. This is also referred to as the mobile washroom trailer.

Video Village: This is an area usually under a tent where the Director and team watch the monitors when filming

Walkie check: Does this radio work properly?

Window Shot (Martini Shot): The last shot of the film day.

What's your 20: What is your location?

Wrap: The filming that day has finished.

Here is some space to write down slang word meanings that are not on this list.

~ SLANG WORDS ~

~ SLANG WORDS ~

~ SLANG WORDS ~

4
Department Names

In this section, I describe each job on set required to produce a film project. There are many more positions that deal with the creating of any production such as administration, scouting, preparing, editing (post-production), and promoting, to name a few. I did not include these positions because this book is for most of the job titles you will see on the actual working film set.

Actors: Study the production script and bring the story to life by acting it out.

ADR (Automated Dialog Replacement)/ Dialog Editors: Control the quality and placement of the actors' dialogue. Rerecord the dialogue later with the actors if required.

Aerial Camera Assistant: This specialized position is responsible for coordinating the proper camera systems to the aircraft used.

Aerial Camera Pilot: Flies the aircraft used to capture any aerial sequences needed. They also fly the on-screen aircraft.

Aerial Director of Photography (DOP): Manages the aerial crew to film the needed elements safely.

Apprentice Lighting Technician: Learns to be a qualified Technician through hours of assisting.

Armorer: Responsible for all weapons and firearms used on set.

Art Director: Gives the look and feel to all locations the production films by realizing the Production Designer's creative vision.

Am I The Idiot?

Assistant Hairdresser: Providing support for the Senior and Chief Hairdressers.

Assistant Location Manager (ALM): Giving support to the Location Manager and directing the location team on each set.

Assistant Make-up Artist: Assists the Senior Make-up staff.

Best Boy: The best electrician in the electronics department led by the Gaffer. A term from "The Gaffers Handbook".

Boom Operator (Boom Op.): Places and operates the boom microphone for the Sound Mixer.

Camera Operator: Prepares and operates the camera with the equipment necessary.

Camera Trainee: Helps the 2nd Assistant Camera to be educated in camera operating.

Catering Crew: Assembles and provides meals for the cast and crew filming on set.

Chief Hairdresser: Designs then executes the hair style of each actor. Also, in charge of the entire hair department.

Chief Make-up Artist: Runs the make-up department to create and apply the proper make-up required for each scene.

Choreographer: Works closely with Directors, Producers, and Designers to create then train the Dancers or Actors on the movements needed.

Console Operator (Dimmer Board Op): Operates the fixed and conventional lights on set.

Costume Assistant: Works to assist with the design and construction of costumes.

Costume Supervisor: This is the main connection for the hair, art, and make-up departments.

Crane Operator: Sets up and operates cranes that carry cameras and crew.

Digital Imaging Technician (DIT): Secures footage to a backup while creating dailies for the Director and DOP to view.

Director: Creates the driving force behind the compilation of the production. Brings the written story to life using the actors and sets.

Director of Photography (DOP): Works with the Director, camera crew, and lighting to create the look of the film.

Drapes-master: Creates and installs all soft furnishings for set design.

Electrics (Juicer, Sparks): Constructs and maintains the electrical needs of the set.

Executive Producer (EP): Completes the film on time and on budget by supervising the department heads.

First Assistant Camera (1st AC or Focus Pullers): Keeps the camera in focus during the filming of each scene.

First Assistant Director (1st AD): This position organizes and executes the shooting schedule. The right hand of the Director who makes sure the departments run smoothly.

Gaffer: Oversees all the technical operations of lighting and electrics producing the proper effects.

Genny Operator Genny Op.: Responsible for all the generators operations and maintenance.

Greensmen (Greens): Fit the script requirements with foliage and greenery.

Grip: Building the equipment that supports the cameras used. They also help move and position the cameras smoothly.

Hairdresser: Oversees the continuity of the actors' hair on set.

Lighting Technician (Sparks): Organizes and sets up the lighting equipment used on each set.

Location Manager (LM): Negotiates fees, permissions, and terms of each location the production films at.

Make-up / Hair Artist: Oversees the continuity of all the hair and makeup of the actors on set.

Make-up / Hair Assistant: Sets up and maintains all work stations for hair and makeup application. Also helps senior staff with continuity.

Make-up / Hair Trainee: Sets up and maintains makeup and hair workstations while observing senior staff to learn on the job.

Make-up Artist: Oversees the makeup continuity including prosthetics and facial hair of the actors.

Marine Diving Camera Crew: Manages and operates all underwater sequences needed in the production.

Moving Light Operator: Operates and maintains all the automated moving lights.

Production Assistant (PA): The starting position for many crew members. Responsible for many jobs including parking and organizing the garbage.

Production Manager (PM): This job makes sure the production works efficiently for the producers.

Production Sound Mixer: Works with the Boom Operator to record clear dialogue.

Prosthetics Artist: All the prosthetic makeup is made and applied by this position.

Puppeteer: Interprets and performs the script by manipulating inanimate objects as the actors.

Rigger: Assembles cables, ropes, scaffolding and all rigging gear.

Script Supervisor (Scripty): Oversees the script being followed by the actors and ensures the continuity of the dialogue during each scene.

Second Assistant Camera: Responsible for the changing of the lenses, batteries, and film used by the camera.

Second Assistant Director (2nd AD): Helps the First AD creates the call sheet, oversees the actors, and timing of makeup/hair between scenes.

Set Decorator (Set Dec): Installs, organizes, and details all the set props needed for each set. Also keeps records of each item before shooting, during shooting, and on packing up for the return when filming is completed.

Sound Assistant: This trainee position aids in general back up for the sound crew.

Standby Art Director: Works during filming on set by observing for the Production Designer.

Standby Carpenter: Fixes or adjusts any wooden structures during filming.

Standby Painter: Is on set to make corrections to any paint requirements needed.

Standby Props: Works with the Art Director to carry out any on the spot tasks, and/or solves last minute problems.

Standby Rigger: Fixes or adjusts last minute problems with rigging equipment.

Steadicam Operator: This camera operator uses the steady camera equipment to keep the shot steady while in motion.

Stunt Performer (Stunts): Takes the actors' place to perform dangerous and specialized actions that are called for by the script.

Third Assistant Director (3rd AD): Supports the 1st AD and 2nd AD on the set or location. Also accountable for organizing the background, vehicles, and crew when needed.

Training Assistant Director (TAD): Helps the 3rd AD keep an eye on the actors required for each scene, plus performing menial tasks like distributing all the radios and batteries to all departments.

Transport Captain: Responsible for the transportation schedule for all cast, key crew, and the work trucks needed at any location.

Transport Co-Captain: Organizes and supports the Transport Captain with the duties required for driving all vehicles within the production.

Unit Driver (Transpo): Transports the artists, cast, crew, and carries out deliveries when required.

Unit Stills Photographer (Stills): This is the person who takes photographs of all film sets, cast, and studio shots.

Wardrobe Supervisor: Oversees the use and day-to-day wardrobe and/or costumes on the film set.

When you are new to a set it is good to write down the name and job title of the people you work with. In this industry you meet a lot of people and it is hard to remember everyone by their name.

~ NAMES ~

~ NAMES ~

~ NAMES ~

~ NAMES ~

5
General Requirements
(FIRST DAY)
(Vancouver, BC, Canada)

Depending on what department you work for, whether you are an actor, or a background actor, will determine what is expected of you. Since there are many different rules and expectations, I will give each their own list of requirements that every new crew member must complete.

I broke down the three positions into their own section to explain the protocol and requirements for each.

-CREW MEMBERS-
Fill Out Your Start Pack
(DEAL MEMO)

When anyone starts to work for a production, the first thing that should be done is to register the proper paperwork called a "Start Pack" with the accounting department so one can get paid. Each production needs a photo copy of your tax assessment and identification.

There are two different ways to register with payroll so the taxes you pay are filed correctly. The most common one used is called an "Individual Start Pack", and this is for a person that is an employee of the production. This means that the production is responsible for submitting the individual's income tax to the government and preparing their record of employment, etc.

The other set of forms is called a "Corporate Start Pack" and is for an individual who subcontracts themselves as a business to the production. These people have registered themselves as a corporation with the government and are responsible for submitting their own tax deductions because they are considered a corporation hired by the production.

It is important to make sure this paperwork is filled out properly and handed in on the first day of work. Besides the legal ramifications that need to be established when one starts work, it is also important to be registered for the production's budget. Once the forms are filled out, they are to be handed in to the AD trailer or "Honey Wagon" so they can be sent to the production office.

Follow Instructions Carefully

This rule is very irritating if it is not followed properly. The way all the departments perform any duty has been predetermined and organized before the location is prepped for filming. The set has been overseen by a group of department heads at an earlier date during a trip they call a "Tech Survey". They map out the equipment and layout needed by their department determined by the direction of the scenes that will be filmed. Every placement and assembly has been well thought out by the people hired to do this job.

It seems obvious to me that my opinion about the setup is irrelevant to the process. Anyone who thinks they are helping by telling their superior a better way to do things is mistaking their opinion as valuable. The one who organizes the placement and distribution of that department's gak was hired to do so and should be trusted to do the right thing, so don't provide your opinion unless you are asked to do so specifically. The more you can follow direction to the letter, the better the result and desired reputation of "easy to work with". This also means you will be called for work more because you can be trusted to achieve the desired outcome. There is no seniority when it comes to film work, so the best people get the best jobs.

The other thing that is a pain when directing a team is when someone on that team 'doesn't finish all the jobs they were asked to do. Sometimes there is a list of things to complete and if anything gets forgotten it can result in delays for the film crew to continue. I found it helpful to have a pad of paper and pen on standby, so I wouldn't just rely on memory.

Proper Work Wear

This is a very important rule that applies to all crew members everyday they are on set. The location and weather are the conditions that each crew member should pay attention to. Preparation for all environments is the key to a good or bad day. I personally have not been dressed for the situation that I was in and soon learned my lesson.

The other thing to be aware of is footwear when working these long days. Everyone should try and find the most comfortable shoes for the hours that will be spent on their feet. Another good piece of advice is to have an extra pair of socks to change into at lunch time or whenever you decide you need a change.

It is not always the case, but some shows film on construction sites, or sewage plants and by law these places require footwear with steel toes, a reflective vest, and hard hat. When this occurs then every crew member on the site should have these things on, no question. The production usually supplies the hard hat and vest, but not the steel toe shoes/boots.

The most important thing to have in Vancouver Canada is rain gear. I learned this was the case when it started to get cold and rainy every day. I know this does not apply in other parts of the world but here it is essential. When the rain gear is combined with warm clothes one can have a relatively comfortable day despite the weather.

-ACTORS-

There are differences between the main actors and the day actors when it comes to rules and expectations. Since the main actors have already been informed of their role in the production by their agent then I will only address the day actors. The rules I list will help the day to run smoother for both crew and actors.

If you drive a car then you must park in the crew park like everyone else in the film crew. The main actors are the only ones that have their own assigned parking most of the time. Never park near set because your car will need to be moved or even towed. The PA at the crew park will make sure you get a shuttle to your trailer so don't worry about walking to set.

The first thing to do when actors arrive at the "Circus" of film trailers is to find the AD office. This is usually in a trailer that has both Men and Women's washrooms as well and is called the "Honey Wagon". The Third AD is the one who situates each actor into their appropriate trailers to prepare for the scenes they are in. They will also make sure the proper paper work is filled out before the actor does anything else.

From that point on the Third AD or TAD are responsible for continually being aware of every actor's progress and location on the set. The task of going to wardrobe, makeup, and hair are specifically timed and organized by the Third AD so the Actor never needs to be concerned about anything except their lines and performance. Following the direction of the Third AD or TAD will make this process run more efficiently and allow the actor time to concentrate on the task at hand.

It is very important to inform the Third AD or the TAD if the Actor must leave the set, even if it is for a short time. If you are called to set and cannot be found, then you are for sure called an Idiot!!

-EXTRAS/BACKGROUND ACTORS-

If you are driving one must be aware of the parking situation because it depends on the location and show. One of the mistakes that many background actors make is to assume that parking their car is always provided by the production. The parking sometimes is limited and the rule that must be followed by the production is to park the union extras only.

If your Background Agent does not know, then you must ask the PA in crew park when arriving on set.

The first thing one should do when going to set from crew park or taking transit, is to find out where BG is to get ready. There should be arrow signs that say "Background", or "BG", that point to the proper area. The people who organize and are responsible for all the extras to be dressed and ready to go to set are called "Background Wranglers". These are the people that all the background actors must locate first when arriving on set and should rely on for all information.

The BG Wranglers will hand out and collect the proper paperwork for payment. Every production needs a photo copy of your tax assessment and your identification. This is not a request but a requirement for a paycheck to be printed so make sure you have this with you. They also direct each person to the wardrobe, hair and/or make up departments to get ready.

Once you have completed all the tasks necessary before you go to the set, it is your duty to be easy to find by the Background Wranglers always. If you must grab something from your car, go for a cigarette, or anything that takes you away from BG holding, you tell the Wrangler every time.

Am I The Idiot?

When you are going to set to film, the BG Wrangler will tell you where to go. When you arrive on set it is usually the First and Second AD who will place you and tell you what to do. The Wranglers and the TAD help if there are bigger numbers of BG to place.

Once you are in place and know what to do then it is a requirement to pay attention to the First AD constantly. Never leave the set to go to the bathroom, have a smoke, or for any other reason without asking the BG Wrangler first. When people on set make assumptions, they run the risk of being considered an Idiot, or worse.

The other thing that will get you into trouble is when a non-union BG Actor eats food from a union Craft Service table, or Catering. The only time that non-union BG Actors can eat from the union food, is when there is a small amount of BG that film day. If this is the case the Wrangler will tell you.

The final thing is the BG Actors are responsible for the wardrobe and/or props given to them. It is essential to make sure the items are returned and recorded. If the shooting is over a few days to a week, the wardrobe you are wearing gets put together and tagged at the end of each day before you leave. Never take anything home promising to bring it back tomorrow. Never ever!!

Basic Advice for BG

It is good to bring your own pen to fill out your paperwork because there is never enough, and you can be waiting to use one for a long time.

I suggest to always follow the background wrangler's word no matter what. Do not ask the person beside you if you are unsure of where to go or what to do. Just like listed in the rules earlier, pay attention and never guess.

The wardrobe you bring to set should be neutral colours with no logo's, designs, stripes, prints, red, white, or black colours of any kind. Each person should have three changes with them for the wardrobe crew to pick through. If specific wardrobe like formal wear, or dated fashion is required then your agent will inform you or it will be provided by the production. It is also good to bring thermal underwear to wear under outfits if shooing exterior and/or at night in Canada.

Do not wear lots of makeup, hair product, perfume/cologne, or facial hair. It is the job of the makeup artist and hair stylist to design the looks needed and it is easier to add something then remove it. If facial hair is needed, then your BG agent should tell you specifically.

My final bit of advice is always keep a good attitude and remembering to have fun! You become more relaxed each time you go to set and therefore one becomes more natural. Sometimes you will work beside big stars and other times you are just sitting in a crowd with other BG actors. I was only fortunate enough to do this part time, but I loved every minute of it!

EPILOGUE

There is no way I can put into words how much I love the film industry that helped me out of a dead-end slump in my life! It turned out that this art form is my passion and therefore the crazy work hours required did not seem to be as painful as one would think. I believe this labor can only be performed by a certain type of person that puts the pride in their work above their own personal comfort. Every one of these exceptional people I was fortunate to work beside are always professional with a great attitude about life that made me feel blessed.

THANK YOU

I would like to thank all the productions and companies that produce films in Vancouver, BC, Canada that I was lucky to work for. I also included the various Companies that helped me with donations and/or deals for my independent filming projects.

- 50/50
- A Mile in His Shoes
- Aries
- Arrow
- Bridge Studios
- Brightlight Pictures
- Chaos
- Dybbuk Box
- Falling Skies
- Fringe
- Koko's Adventures
- Matrix
- Mission Impossible - Ghost Protocol

Michael Parnall

- Normal
- Parallel Rentals
- PS Lighting
- Psych
- Reaper
- Revolution
- Robo Cop (2014)
- Smallville
- Stargate Atlantis
- Supernatural
- The Company You Keep
- The Day the Earth Stood Still
- The Interview
- The Killing
- The Last Fall of Ashes
- The L Word
- The Watchmen
- The X Files: I Want to Believe
- To the Mat
- Untold Stories of the ER
- Wayward Pines
- When Calls the Heart
- William F. Whites Inc.
- William F. Whites Inc. - LES Vancouver

Am I The Idiot?

There are many outstanding people I would like to thank as well. These people are cemented in my memory because every one of them helped me in one way or another. I would like every person on this list to know how much I appreciate the time I spent working with them and all the information I learned from their wisdom. Anyone who knows or works with these people is truly blessed!

- A.A Wintringham
- Adam Ferguson
- Adiam Asrat
- Aiden Wilson
- Alex Seymour
- Allan Ross
- Allison Spicer
- Amanda Athena Blue
- Amanda Connache
- Amanda Murphy
- Andrea Connacher
- Andres Salas
- Andrew McClean
- Andrew Shirley
- Anna McBarron
- Antonio Hunnisett
- Anya Gadison
- Ariel Carefoot
- Art Seto
- Attila Vaski
- Beth Henderson
- Beth Charlesworth
- Bill Burns
- Bill Davies
- Blake Norman
- Blake Vanderheyden
- Bobby Mensah
- Bonnie Northcott
- Brad Kita
- Bren MacDonald
- Brendan Wilson
- Brian Dyck
- Brian Hulme
- Byron Kopman
- Cameron Gardner
- Carl Roulston
- Carol Marks George
- Cat Renee

Michael Parnall

Cathrine Owen
Catou Kearney
Chris West
Chris Furanna
Chris Howarth
Chris Moone
Christa Anderson
Cliff Kosterman
Conrad Janze
Corinne Clark
Corinne Lea
Corrie Alexander
Craig Forrest
Crysta Delaplace
Dan Moore
Daniel Bruce
Daniel Mathias
Darlene Choo
Darren Kelly
Darryl Griffiths
David Costello
David Halifax
David Tamkin
Dax Belanger
Derek Rodger
Devin Schule
Devina Faye
Dominic Wutz

Dylan Kilgor
Elizabeth Seymour
Elyse Levesque
Emma Peterson
Fiona Crossley
Fluffy
Geoff Dodd
Giovanna Morales Vargas
Greta Schel
Grizz Salzl
Hanna George
Hans Daval
Hayley Read
Hester Bloom
Isis Oliveira
Ivette Hernandez
Jack McQuistin
James Bamford
James McPhee
Janice Gill
Janice Yip
Janet Robertson
Jannat Deol
Jason Cox
Jason Fisher
Jason Momoa
Jason Pawlett
Jay Robbins

Am I The Idiot?

Jennifer Adamson
Jessica Alley
Jessica Cheung M.D.
Jina Johnson-Ryan
Jitka Dermiskova
Jodi-Lynn Boulton
John Braico
Jon Cairns
Jordan Ryan
Josey Wiesmen
Justin DeLima
Justin Turnbull
Kai Kennedy
Kameron Bodaly
Kana Sawamoto
Karen Bushnell
Karl Baheena
Karyn Jackson
Katie Ewasiuk
Kayla LaSaga
Kayvon Saremi
Kelly Hudson
Kelly Shea
Kevin Parks
Kevin Royce
Kevin Schultz
Khang Nguyen
Kheyann Hance

Kimball Jansma
Kipp Lightburn
Kirk Adamson
Kirk Jaques
Kohl Jones
Konrad Wieclawski
Kris McRonney
Krysten Merrick
Kyle James-Patrick
Lake Hughes
Larie Stoley
Larry Portman
Lauren Beason
Lauren Michelle
Leland Giffen
Linda McClean
Lou Bollo
Louis Ferreira
Lydia Strojin
Marco Piovesan
Marion Pejaire
Mark Bonker
Mark Richards
Max Noel
Megan Dawson
Meggs
Michael Bendner
Michael Bishop

Michael Parnall

Mike Campbell
Mike Howorun
Michael Hauka
Michael J. Paik
Michael Marshal
Michelle Cornish
Milton Yet Chow Ng
Moe Barr
Nami Khasho
Nancy Na
Natalie Hoskins
Nick Dent
Nicky Wilke
Patricia Anderson
Patrick Ramsay
Patti Props
Paul Bronfman
Paul Potvin
Pedro Eugenio
Peter Klamis
Rachael Pilas
Rachael Taylor
Rachel Smyth
Rae Clark
Reba Rowe
Richard Tickner
Rick Dobran
Rico Mieinicki

Rob Amar
Robert Clark
Robert Carlyle
Ron French
Ron Hrynuik
Roland Pointner
Rory Brett
Rosie Brown
Russ Hamilton
Samantha Baskerville
Sarah Hansen
Sarah Lentz
Sarah Rayner
Sean Finnan
Sean Meade
Shawn Flynn
Sean Williamson
Shane C. Lennox
Shannon O'Neal
Sebastian Portman
Stace Synkiw
Sukh Sing
Tammie Barker
Taylor Milne
Teresa Margaret King
Terry Wong
Tiffany Timms
Tim Day

Am I The Idiot?

Toby Hargrave
Toddy P
Tom Crowe
Ty Lowe
Viv Pfeffer
Warren Fulton
Wayne Toews
William Sleepy
Willie Lavendale
Zay Bringnal

NOTES

NOTES

NOTES

NOTES

ABOUT THE AUTHOR

Michael Parnall has worked in the film industry for more than ten years and like all new members was considered an idiot at first. His background acting, and production assistant work led him to opportunities working for a movie studio, and a rental business dedicated to the film industry. Years spent in these environments gave him the proper connections he needed to shoot his own short film productions. Besides writing and directing his own independent film projects, he volunteered his time to help fellow independent film makers as well.

Since his diagnosis he is unable to work in the industry that he loved to be a part of. Medical challenges have not stopped his will to be creative and he continues with imaginative writing.

www.ingramcontent.com/pod-product-compliance
Lightning Source LLC
LaVergne TN
LVHW011737060526
838200LV00051B/3211